Gourmet Dog Biscuits

Carole Horstmeyer is also author of:

Howl-iday Dog Biscuits

Gourmet Cat Treats

Dog Party!

Gourmet Dog Biscuits

A Cookbook of Tasty Treats for Your Favorite Fido

by **Carole Horstmeyer**

Published by
CRAFTS AND CRE-"ATE"-TIONS
St. Louis, Missouri

Note:
The recipes appearing in this book have been carefully tested. However, there is no guarantee. The author/publisher cannot be responsible for human error or typographical errors. Your results may vary. The author/publisher cannot assume liability for the information presented herein or for unfavorable results.
If you have any questions about the suitability of these recipes for your dog(s), please consult your veterinarian.
Children should always cook/bake with adult supervision.
These recipes are not intended for human consumption.

Copyright ©1996 by Carole Horstmeyer
All rights reserved.

No portion of this book may be reproduced or used in any form or by any means, mechanical, or electronic, including photocopying, recording, or by any information retrieval or storage system, without written permission from the publisher.

Published by Crafts and Cre-"ate"-tions
P.O. Box 190195
St. Louis, MO 63119

"Whole Wheat Dog Biscuits" and "Garlic Dog Biscuits" previously appeared in Crafts and Cre-"ate"-tions™ Newsletter (another publication by this author).

Library of Congress Catalog Card Number: 96-96739

ISBN 0-9653216-0-6

Printed in the United States of America

Fourth Printing

SPECIAL THANKS to:

MOM - for her unwavering support

PEARL SELF - for her proofreading and editorial expertise

CATHY VANDERHEYDEN - for her assistance in designing the front cover

DR. W. - for the care of my four-legged friends

BARON - for his unselfish participation as taste tester

- - - - - -

The crew at **SHOW ME ST. LOUIS:**

DEBBYE, JOHN & JORDAN

Thanks for having me as a guest on your show!
I really enjoy working with you!

TABLE OF CONTENTS

INTRODUCTION	5
POINTERS	8
GRAIN VARIETIES	
Whole Wheat	13
Rye	15
FRUIT FLAVORS	
Apple-Cinnamon	19
Apple-Raisin	21
Banana	23
Orange	25
Tropical	27
SPICE FLAVORS	
"Nice" Spice	31
Oatmeal-Cinnamon	33
HERB FLAVORS	
Dill Weed	37
Herb Medley	39
Parsley	41
CAROB FLAVORS	
Carob-Peanut Butter	45
Carob Temptations	47

PEANUT BUTTER FLAVORS
Banana-Peanut Butter	**51**
Peanut Butter	**53**
Peanut Butter & Jelly	**55**

MEAT FLAVORS
"Chipped" Beef Jerky	**59**
Liver Snacks	**61**
Vegetable-Beef Flavor	**63**

SPECIALTY FLAVORS
Barbecue-Flavor	**67**
Cheese-Flavor	**69**
Garlic	**71**
"Grandma's"	**73**
Pizza-Flavor	**75**

INDEX   79

ABOUT THE AUTHOR   80

INTRODUCTION

The first versions of my gourmet dog biscuits (Whole Wheat and Garlic) appeared in my newsletter - **CRAFTS AND CRE-"ATE"-TIONS**. When I later shared these recipes with the viewers of a live, local TV show (Show Me St. Louis), I realized, based on the number of requests, how popular the recipes are. I was still receiving requests for the dog biscuit recipes almost five months after I first shared them on TV!

I also found the dog biscuits to be very popular among my "dog network." After giving various flavors of dog biscuits to friends and dog club members for their dogs, it was not unusual for me to hear them say that their dogs would not touch a dog biscuit bought at the store, but their dog would eat the homemade biscuits and not leave a crumb!

The inspiration for the additional dog biscuit flavors came from a variety of sources. Baron, my German Shepherd, lets me know very clearly what he likes. When I eat an orange, Baron appears immediately; this served as the inspiration for the orange-flavored dog biscuits.

Baron also lets me know what he doesn't like. One version of the apple-flavored dog biscuits was a flop - Baron spit them out. After a revision, these Apple-Cinnamon Dog Biscuits became one of his favorites.

As I ate "people food" I was always considering how I could convert it to "dog treats." This served as the inspiration for the flavors like barbecue, and pizza.

Chocolate is one of my favorite things. However, chocolate contains a substance which is toxic to dogs. The solution...carob dog biscuits.

The Whole Wheat Dog Biscuit serves as the basic recipe for many of the varieties and flavors. Once you have mastered this easy recipe, the other versions are a snap to make. This recipe creates a hard, crunchy dog biscuit.

If your dog does not prefer hard dog biscuits, there are several less crunchy versions: look for Oatmeal-Cinnamon Dog Biscuits, "Chipped" Beef Jerky Dog Biscuits, or "Grandma's" Dog Biscuits.

Gourmet Dog Biscuits

These gourmet dog biscuits are inexpensive, easy to make and wholesome - the biscuits have no added salt or preservatives. In addition, most of the biscuits have no added sugar. If your dog is on a **low-sodium diet** or has **heart disease**, please be aware that there may be salt or sodium in some of the ingredients used in the recipes.

Please keep in mind that these dog biscuits are meant to serve as a treat and are not meant to replace a dog's regular diet. It is best to give your dog small amounts of the biscuits at first, to be sure the biscuit agrees with your dog's stomach.

Also remember that, just as people prefer certain foods over other foods, some dogs prefer certain flavors over other flavors.

If your dog is on a special diet or if you have any questions about the suitability of these dog biscuits for your dog(s), please consult your veterinarian.

I hope you enjoy making these dog biscuits as much as I do. I also hope your dog enjoys them as much as Baron does.

BONE APPETITE!!   *Carole*

POINTERS

Cookie Cutters

Look for dog-bone shaped cookie cutters at craft stores and in the cookie cutter section of specialty kitchen shops.

There are a variety of dog-bone shaped cookie cutters available. The cookie cutters come in many sizes, from 1 ½ inches long to 3 or more inches long. Some cookie cutters are made of metal and some are made of plastic. I have used both varieties with success.

Use smaller size cookie cutters for biscuits for small dogs and the larger size cookie cutters for biscuits for large dogs.

Baking

To ensure even baking of the biscuits, rotate the cookie sheets about halfway through the baking process. That is, move the cookie sheet on the top rack to the bottom rack, and the cookie sheet on the bottom rack to the top rack.

Monitor the baking time carefully. Smaller biscuits take less time to bake than larger biscuits.

POINTERS (cont.)

Ingredients

The various types of flour used in the recipes (unbleached, whole wheat, rye) are available in most grocery stores.

If you don't have "fresh broth" you may use bouillon cubes or bouillon granules (following the instructions on the package) to make broth. Be sure to allow the broth to cool completely before using.

Look in health food stores for the carob powder used in the carob variations of dog biscuits.

(Note: All temperatures for baking are given in Fahrenheit.)

GRAIN VARIETIES

This recipe uses wholesome ingredients and has no added salt or sugar. The whole wheat version makes a hard, crunchy dog biscuit.

This is the first dog biscuit recipe which I created. Once you have mastered this simple recipe the other versions are a snap to make, since this is the basic recipe used in a variety of the other flavors.

Gourmet Dog Biscuits

WHOLE WHEAT DOG BISCUITS

1 ½ cups unbleached flour
1 ½ cups whole wheat flour
½ cup cornmeal
⅛ cup nonfat dry milk
1 egg, slightly beaten
1 to 1 ¼ cups of water or broth

1. Stir together the dry ingredients in a large bowl. Add the egg, then add the water or broth gradually, stirring with a wooden spoon. The dough should be very stiff; if not, add a little more flour. Knead the dough with your hands to create a smooth texture.
2. Roll the dough ¼ inch thick. (It helps if the "top" and "bottom" of the dough are lightly floured.) Use the cookie cutter to cut out the biscuits. Place the biscuits about ½ inch apart on lightly greased cookie sheets.
3. Bake in a pre-heated 350 degree oven for about 45 minutes to one hour. The biscuits should be lightly browned and they should not be moist inside. Turn the oven off and let the biscuits stay inside without opening the oven door for five hours, or overnight, to let them harden.

Store in an airtight container.

MAKES: ABOUT 4 DOZEN - 3" x 1" BISCUITS.

This recipe takes advantage of the full-bodied taste and smell of rye flour.

This version creates a very stiff dough. Be ready to use some muscle power to roll out the dough. The completed dog biscuits look and smell so wholesome!

With the way Baron sometimes tries to get attention, I guess when he eats one of these biscuits, he is "ham" and rye!

Gourmet Dog Biscuits

RYE DOG BISCUITS

1 ½ cups rye flour
1 cup whole wheat flour
1 cup unbleached flour
¼ cup cornmeal
¼ cup nonfat dry milk
1 egg, slightly beaten
1 to 1 ¼ cups of water

1. Stir together the dry ingredients in a large bowl. Add the egg, then add the water gradually, stirring with a wooden spoon. The dough should be very stiff; if not, add a little more flour. Knead the dough with your hands to create a smooth texture.
2. Roll the dough ¼ inch thick. (It helps if the "top" and "bottom" of the dough are lightly floured.) Use the cookie cutter to cut out the biscuits. Place the biscuits about ½ inch apart on lightly greased cookie sheets.
3. Bake in a pre-heated 350 degree oven for about 45 minutes to one hour. The biscuits should be lightly browned and they should not be moist inside. Turn the oven off and let the biscuits stay inside without opening the oven door for five hours, or overnight, to let them harden.

Store in an airtight container.

MAKES: ABOUT 3½ DOZEN - 3" x 1" BISCUITS.

FRUIT FLAVORS

This is one of Baron's top two favorites! It is ironic because the first variation of this recipe was so awful that Baron wouldn't even eat them! He spit them out! (I think there was too much applesauce in the recipe, but Baron was too polite to say so.)

Luckily (for him and for me), I didn't give up. The second try was perfect. He loves them!!

Gourmet Dog Biscuits

APPLE-CINNAMON DOG BISCUITS

1 ½ cups unbleached flour
1 ½ cups whole wheat flour
½ cup cornmeal
⅛ cup nonfat dry milk
2 teaspoons ground cinnamon
½ cup smooth applesauce
1 egg, slightly beaten
½ to ¾ cup of water

1. Stir together the dry ingredients in a large bowl. Add the applesauce and egg, and blend thoroughly. Then add the water gradually, stirring with a wooden spoon. The dough should be very stiff; if not, add a little more flour. Knead the dough with your hands to create a smooth texture.
2. Roll the dough ¼ inch thick. (It helps if the "top" and "bottom" of the dough are lightly floured.) Use the cookie cutter to cut out the biscuits. Place the biscuits about ½ inch apart on lightly greased cookie sheets.
3. Bake in a pre-heated 350 degree oven for about 38 to 50 minutes. The biscuits should be lightly browned and they should not be moist inside. Turn the oven off and let the biscuits stay inside without opening the oven door for five hours, or overnight, to let them harden.

Store in an airtight container.

MAKES: ABOUT 4 DOZEN - 3" x 1" BISCUITS.

These biscuits have the added touch of raisins.

When you cut the biscuits out with the cookie cutter, be sure that there are no raisins sticking out of the sides of the biscuits -- if there are, the raisins will burn while baking.

Since this book was first published, some research has indicated that LARGE amounts of raisins may be toxic to dogs. If you have any questions about acceptable amounts of raisins for your dog(s), please consult your veterinarian.

Gourmet Dog Biscuits

APPLE-RAISIN DOG BISCUITS

1 ½ cups unbleached flour
1 ½ cups whole wheat flour
½ cup cornmeal
⅜ cup nonfat dry milk
½ cup smooth applesauce
½ cup raisins (preferably "baking" raisins which are more moist)
1 egg, slightly beaten
¾ cup of water

1. Stir together the dry ingredients in a large bowl. Add the applesauce and raisins and blend well. Add the egg, then add the water gradually, stirring with a wooden spoon. The dough should be very stiff; if not, add a little more flour. Knead the dough with your hands to create a smooth texture.
2. Roll the dough ¼ inch thick. (It helps if the "top" and "bottom" of the dough are lightly floured.) Use the cookie cutter to cut out the biscuits. (Be sure to trim or remove any raisins that stick out of the sides of the biscuits before baking.) Place the biscuits about ½ inch apart on lightly greased cookie sheets.
3. Bake in a pre-heated 350 degree oven for about 45 minutes to one hour. The biscuits should be lightly browned and they should not be moist inside. Turn the oven off and let the biscuits stay inside without opening the oven door for five hours, or overnight, to let them harden.

Store in an airtight container in the refrigerator.

MAKES: ABOUT 4 DOZEN - 3" x 1" BISCUITS.

Whenever I would eat a banana, Baron would suddenly appear. It didn't take long to figure out that he loves bananas.

I decided that if bananas could be put into banana bread, they could also be put into dog biscuits. Baron agrees.

Ripe bananas work well in this recipe.

Gourmet Dog Biscuits

BANANA DOG BISCUITS

1 ½ cups unbleached flour
1 ½ cups whole wheat flour
½ cup cornmeal
⅛ cup nonfat dry milk
½ cup mashed ripe banana (about 1 banana)
1 egg, slightly beaten
¾ to 1 cup of water

1. Stir together the dry ingredients in a large bowl. Add the mashed banana and egg; stir until well blended. Then add the water gradually, stirring with a wooden spoon. The dough should be very stiff; if not, add a little more flour. Knead the dough with your hands to create a smooth texture.
2. Roll the dough ¼ inch thick. (It helps if the "top" and "bottom" of the dough are lightly floured.) Use the cookie cutter to cut out the biscuits. Place the biscuits about ½ inch apart on lightly greased cookie sheets.
3. Bake in a pre-heated 350 degree oven for about 45 minutes to one hour. The biscuits should be lightly browned and they should not be moist inside. Turn the oven off and let the biscuits stay inside without opening the oven door for five hours, or overnight, to let them harden.

Store in an airtight container.

MAKES: ABOUT 5 DOZEN - 3" x 1" BISCUITS.

In the same way that Baron magically appears when I eat a banana, he also gives me the "I want some, too" stare when I eat an orange.

That hungry look is the inspiration for the orange-flavored biscuits.

Gourmet Dog Biscuits

ORANGE DOG BISCUITS

1 ½ cups unbleached flour
1 ½ cups whole wheat flour
½ cup cornmeal
⅛ cup nonfat dry milk
1 egg, slightly beaten
1 to 1 ¼ cups of orange juice

1. Stir together the dry ingredients in a large bowl. Add the egg, then add the orange juice gradually, stirring with a wooden spoon. The dough should be very stiff; if not, add a little more flour. Knead the dough with your hands to create a smooth texture.
2. Roll the dough ¼ inch thick. (It helps if the "top" and "bottom" of the dough are lightly floured.) Use the cookie cutter to cut out the biscuits. Place the biscuits about ½ inch apart on lightly greased cookie sheets.
3. Bake in a pre-heated 350 degree oven for about 45 minutes to one hour. The biscuits should be lightly browned and they should not be moist inside. Turn the oven off and let the biscuits stay inside without opening the oven door for five hours, or overnight, to let them harden.

Store in an airtight container.

MAKES: ABOUT 4 DOZEN - 3" x 1" BISCUITS.

I decided that if the flavors of orange and banana were good solo, then they should be twice as good together!

This unusual combination of flavors is easy to achieve.

Gourmet Dog Biscuits

TROPICAL DOG BISCUITS

1 ½ cups unbleached flour
1 ½ cups whole wheat flour
½ cup cornmeal
½ cup mashed ripe banana (about 1 banana)
1 egg, slightly beaten
¾ to 1 cup of orange juice

1. Stir together the dry ingredients in a large bowl. Add the mashed banana and egg; mix well. Then add the orange juice gradually, stirring with a wooden spoon. The dough should be very stiff; if not, add a little more flour. Knead the dough with your hands to create a smooth texture.
2. Roll the dough ¼ inch thick. (It helps if the "top" and "bottom" of the dough are lightly floured.) Use the cookie cutter to cut out the biscuits. Place the biscuits about ½ inch apart on lightly greased cookie sheets.
3. Bake in a pre-heated 350 degree oven for about 45 minutes to one hour. The biscuits should be lightly browned and they should not be moist inside. Turn the oven off and let the biscuits stay inside without opening the oven door for five hours, or overnight, to let them harden.

Store in an airtight container.

MAKES: ABOUT 5 DOZEN - 3" x 1" BISCUITS.

SPICE FLAVORS

This recipe combines some great flavors often found in spice cookies.

These biscuits make the house smell wonderful while they're baking.

Gourmet Dog Biscuits

"NICE" SPICE DOG BISCUITS

1 ½ cups unbleached flour
1 ½ cups whole wheat flour
½ cup cornmeal
⅛ cup nonfat dry milk
1 teaspoon ground cinnamon
1 teaspoon ground nutmeg
1 ½ teaspoons ground allspice
1 egg, slightly beaten
1 to 1 ¼ cup of water

1. Stir together the dry ingredients in a large bowl. Add the egg, then add the water gradually, stirring with a wooden spoon. The dough should be very stiff; if not, add a little more flour. Knead the dough with your hands to create a smooth texture.
2. Roll the dough ¼ inch thick. (It helps if the "top" and "bottom" of the dough are lightly floured.) Use the cookie cutter to cut out the biscuits. Place the biscuits about ½ inch apart on lightly greased cookie sheets.
3. Bake in a pre-heated 350 degree oven for about 45 minutes to one hour. The biscuits should be lightly browned and they should not be moist inside. Turn the oven off and let the biscuits stay inside without opening the oven door for five hours, or overnight, to let them harden.

Store in an airtight container.

MAKES: ABOUT 4 DOZEN - 3" x 1" BISCUITS.

This is one of Baron's top two favorites. I must admit they smell wonderful, even to my human nose.

These biscuits are not as hard and crunchy as some of the other varieties. If your dog doesn't like hard dog biscuits, you might try this recipe. Even if your dog likes very crunchy biscuits, this recipe can be very tempting.

Gourmet Dog Biscuits

OATMEAL-CINNAMON DOG BISCUITS

¾ cup uncooked "old fashioned" oats (not instant)
¼ cup vegetable oil
1 cup hot water
1 egg, slightly beaten
1 cup whole wheat flour
1 ½ cups unbleached flour
2 teaspoons ground cinnamon

1. Combine the oats, vegetable oil and hot water in a large mixing bowl. Let stand for five minutes.
2. Add the egg, whole wheat flour, unbleached flour and cinnamon to the oat mixture. Stir the ingredients together until blended.
3. The dough should be very stiff; if not, add a little more flour. Knead the dough with your hands for several minutes to create a smooth texture.
4. Roll the dough ¼ inch thick. (It helps if the "top" and "bottom" of the dough are lightly floured.) Use the cookie cutter to cut out the biscuits. Place the biscuits about ½ inch apart on lightly greased cookie sheets.
5. Bake in a pre-heated 300 degree oven for about 1 hour and 25 minutes or so. The biscuits should be lightly browned and they should not be moist inside. Remove the biscuits from the oven and let them cool completely.

Store in an airtight container in the refrigerator.

MAKES: ABOUT 4 DOZEN - 3" x 1" BISCUITS.

HERB FLAVORS

Dill weed is one of those tiny herbs that is big on flavor. It adds both a nice flavor and appearance to the dog biscuits.

Gourmet Dog Biscuits

DILL WEED DOG BISCUITS

1 ½ cups unbleached flour
1 ½ cups whole wheat flour
½ cup cornmeal
⅜ cup nonfat dry milk
2 tablespoons (dried) dill weed
1 egg, slightly beaten
1 to 1 ¼ cups of water

1. Stir together the dry ingredients in a large bowl. Add the egg, then add the water gradually, stirring with a wooden spoon. The dough should be very stiff; if not, add a little more flour. Knead the dough with your hands to create a smooth texture.
2. Roll the dough ¼ inch thick. (It helps if the "top" and "bottom" of the dough are lightly floured.) Use the cookie cutter to cut out the biscuits. Place the biscuits about ½ inch apart on lightly greased cookie sheets.
3. Bake in a pre-heated 350 degree oven for about 45 minutes to one hour. The biscuits should be lightly browned and they should not be moist inside. Turn the oven off and let the biscuits stay inside without opening the oven door for five hours, or overnight, to let them harden.

Store in an airtight container.

MAKES: ABOUT 4 DOZEN - 3" x 1" BISCUITS.

This recipe uses some wonderful herbs.

Cooking tip - Adding dried herbs to a recipe:

Crumble the herbs between your thumb and fingers as you add them to release the most flavor.

Gourmet Dog Biscuits

HERB MEDLEY DOG BISCUITS

1 ½ cups unbleached flour
1 ½ cups whole wheat flour
½ cup cornmeal
⅛ cup nonfat dry milk
2 teaspoons dried thyme
2 teaspoons dried basil
1 egg, slightly beaten
1 to 1 ¼ cups of water

1. Stir together the dry ingredients in a large bowl. Add the egg, then add the water gradually, stirring with a wooden spoon. The dough should be very stiff; if not, add a little more flour. Knead the dough with your hands to create a smooth texture.
2. Roll the dough ¼ inch thick. (It helps if the "top" and "bottom" of the dough are lightly floured.) Use the cookie cutter to cut out the biscuits. Place the biscuits about ½ inch apart on lightly greased cookie sheets.
3. Bake in a pre-heated 350 degree oven for about 45 minutes to one hour. The biscuits should be lightly browned and they should not be moist inside. Turn the oven off and let the biscuits stay inside without opening the oven door for five hours, or overnight, to let them harden.

Store in an airtight container.

MAKES: ABOUT 4 DOZEN - 3" x 1" BISCUITS.

When you want to add a little variety to the dog biscuits, this is an easy variation to try. These biscuits look very attractive with the accent of parsley.

Gourmet Dog Biscuits

PARSLEY DOG BISCUITS

1 ½ cups unbleached flour
1 ½ cups whole wheat flour
½ cup cornmeal
⅛ cup nonfat dry milk
3 tablespoons dried parsley flakes
1 egg, slightly beaten
1 to 1 ¼ cups of water or broth

1. Stir together the dry ingredients in a large bowl. Add the egg, then add the water or broth gradually, stirring with a wooden spoon. The dough should be very stiff; if not, add a little more flour. Knead the dough with your hands to create a smooth texture.
2. Roll the dough ¼ inch thick. (It helps if the "top" and "bottom" of the dough are lightly floured.) Use the cookie cutter to cut out the biscuits. Place the biscuits about ½ inch apart on lightly greased cookie sheets.
3. Bake in a pre-heated 350 degree oven for about 45 minutes to one hour. The biscuits should be lightly browned and they should not be moist inside. Turn the oven off and let the biscuits stay inside without opening the oven door for five hours, or overnight, to let them harden.

Store in an airtight container.

MAKES: ABOUT 4 DOZEN - 3" x 1" BISCUITS.

CAROB FLAVORS

These biscuits use carob and peanut butter to create a great combination of flavors.

These biscuits are a dark, rich brown color accented with specks of peanut butter.

Because chocolate contains a substance which is toxic to dogs, do <u>not</u> use cocoa powder or chocolate in recipes for dogs.

Gourmet Dog Biscuits

CAROB-PEANUT BUTTER DOG BISCUITS

1 ½ cups unbleached flour
1 ½ cups whole wheat flour
½ cup cornmeal
⅜ cup nonfat dry milk
¼ cup carob powder (NOT cocoa powder)
1 egg, slightly beaten
¼ cup creamy peanut butter
2 tablespoons honey
1 cup of water

1. Stir together the dry ingredients in a large bowl. Add the egg, peanut butter and honey. Mix with a pastry blender until the peanut butter is the size of small peas. Then add the water gradually, stirring with a wooden spoon. The dough should be very stiff; if not, add a little more flour. Knead the dough with your hands to create a smooth texture.
2. Roll the dough ¼ inch thick. (It helps if the "top" and "bottom" of the dough are lightly floured.) Use the cookie cutter to cut out the biscuits. Place the biscuits about ½ inch apart on lightly greased cookie sheets.
3. Bake in a pre-heated 350 degree oven for about 35 minutes or so. The biscuits should not be moist inside. Turn the oven off and let the biscuits stay inside without opening the oven door for five hours, or overnight, to let them harden.

Store in an airtight container in the refrigerator.

MAKES: ABOUT 5 DOZEN - 3" x 1" BISCUITS.

Since chocolate contains a substance (theobromine) which is toxic to dogs, do NOT use cocoa powder or chocolate in any recipes for your dog.

Carob, sold in health food stores, is often used as a "substitute" for chocolate. When used for baking, carob powder has a texture very similar to cocoa powder. The taste is similar to chocolate, although somewhat sweeter.

After baking, these biscuits are a deep rich brown color which resembles chocolate.

Gourmet Dog Biscuits

CAROB TEMPTATIONS DOG BISCUITS

2 cups unbleached flour
1 ½ cups whole wheat flour
⅛ cup nonfat dry milk
¼ cup carob powder (<u>NOT</u> cocoa powder)
1 egg, slightly beaten
2 tablespoons honey
1 cup of water

1. Stir together the dry ingredients in a large bowl. Add the egg and honey, then add the water gradually, stirring with a wooden spoon. The dough should be very stiff; if not, add a little more flour. Knead the dough with your hands to create a smooth texture.
2. Roll the dough ¼ inch thick. (It helps if the "top" and "bottom" of the dough are lightly floured.) Use the cookie cutter to cut out the biscuits. Place the biscuits about ½ inch apart on lightly greased cookie sheets.
3. Bake in a pre-heated 350 degree oven for about 35 minutes or so. The biscuits should not be moist inside. Turn the oven off and let the biscuits stay inside without opening the oven door for five hours, or overnight, to let them harden.

Store in an airtight container.

MAKES: ABOUT 4 DOZEN - 3" x 1" BISCUITS.

PEANUT BUTTER FLAVORS

I came up with the idea for these biscuits on Elvis Presley's birthday.

If this combination of flavors was good enough for a sandwich for "The King" -- it's good enough for biscuits for my "Baron."

Gourmet Dog Biscuits

BANANA-PEANUT BUTTER DOG BISCUITS

1 ½ cups unbleached flour
1 ½ cups whole wheat flour
½ cup cornmeal
⅜ cup nonfat dry milk
1 egg, slightly beaten
¼ cup mashed ripe banana (about ½ banana)
¼ cup creamy peanut butter
¾ to 1 cup of water

1. Stir together the dry ingredients in a large bowl. Add the egg, banana, and the peanut butter. Blend well with a pastry blender until peanut butter and banana are about the size of small peas. Add the water gradually, stirring with a wooden spoon. The dough should be very stiff; if not, add a little more flour. Knead the dough with your hands to create a smooth texture.
2. Roll the dough ¼ inch thick. (It helps if the "top" and "bottom" of the dough are lightly floured.) Use the cookie cutter to cut out the biscuits. Place the biscuits about ½ inch apart on lightly greased cookie sheets.
3. Bake in a pre-heated 350 degree oven for about 40 minutes to one hour. The biscuits should be lightly browned and they should not be moist inside. Turn the oven off and let the biscuits stay inside without opening the oven door for five hours, or overnight, to let them harden.

Store in an airtight container in the refrigerator.

MAKES: ABOUT 3½ DOZEN - 3" x 1" BISCUITS.

Peanut butter adds a special flavor to these dog biscuits. For some reason, peanut butter is one of those flavors that many dogs seem to like.

Be sure to use creamy peanut butter!

Use a pastry blender to easily blend the peanut butter with the other ingredients.

Gourmet Dog Biscuits

PEANUT BUTTER DOG BISCUITS

1 ½ cups unbleached flour
1 ½ cups whole wheat flour
½ cup cornmeal
⅜ cup nonfat dry milk
1 egg, slightly beaten
¼ cup creamy peanut butter
1 to 1 ¼ cups of water

1. Stir together the dry ingredients in a large bowl. Add the egg, then the peanut butter. Mix with a pastry blender until the peanut butter is the size of small peas. Add the water gradually, stirring with a wooden spoon. The dough should be very stiff; if not, add a little more flour. Knead the dough with your hands to create a smooth texture.
2. Roll the dough ¼ inch thick. (It helps if the "top" and "bottom" of the dough are lightly floured.) Use the cookie cutter to cut out the biscuits. Place the biscuits about ½ inch apart on lightly greased cookie sheets.
3. Bake in a pre-heated 350 degree oven for about 45 minutes to one hour. The biscuits should be lightly browned and they should not be moist inside. Turn the oven off and let the biscuits stay inside without opening the oven door for five hours, or overnight, to let them harden.

Store in an airtight container in the refrigerator.

MAKES: ABOUT 5 DOZEN - 3" x 1" BISCUITS.

Whenever I think of peanut butter and jelly, I think of lunches in the school cafeteria.

If your dog went to obedience school (or even if your dog didn't), then he or she deserves these, too!

I make tiny biscuits (with a ½" x 1½" dog biscuit cookie cutter) to use as rewards during dog training sessions.

Gourmet Dog Biscuits

PEANUT BUTTER & JELLY DOG BISCUITS

1½ cups unbleached flour
1½ cups whole wheat flour
½ cup cornmeal
⅛ cup nonfat dry milk
2 tablespoons grape jelly
1 egg, slightly beaten
¼ cup creamy peanut butter
¾ to 1 cup water

1. Stir together the dry ingredients in a large bowl. Melt the grape jelly in a small saucepan over medium heat, stirring frequently until completely melted. Remove from heat and let cool.
2. Add the egg, peanut butter and cooled grape jelly to dry ingredients. Mix with a pastry blender until the peanut butter is the size of small peas. Then add the water gradually, stirring with a wooden spoon. The dough should be very stiff; if not, add a little more flour. Knead the dough with your hands to create a smooth texture.
3. Roll the dough ¼ inch thick. (It helps if the "top" and "bottom" of the dough are lightly floured.) Use the cookie cutter to cut out the biscuits. Place the biscuits about ½ inch apart on lightly greased cookie sheets.
4. Bake in a pre-heated 350 degree oven for about 40 minutes to one hour. The biscuits should be lightly browned and they should not be moist inside. Turn the oven off and let the biscuits stay inside without opening the oven door for five hours, or overnight, to let them harden.

Store in an airtight container in the refrigerator.

MAKES: ABOUT 5 DOZEN - 3" x 1" BISCUITS.

MEAT FLAVORS

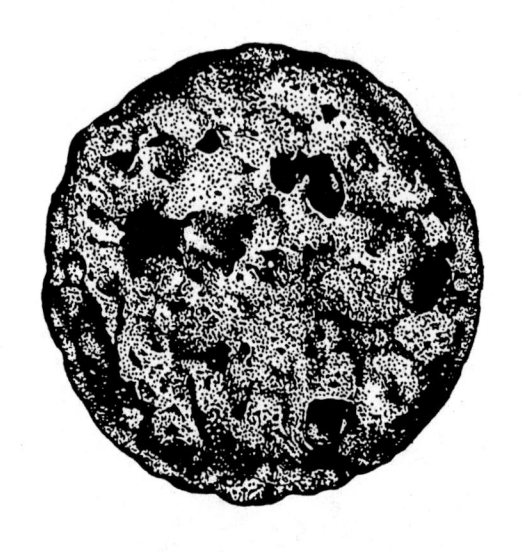

One Christmas, a friend of mine left some goodies on my front porch. As I opened the bag of treats, I thought that she had given me some of the ugliest Fig Newtons® that I had ever seen. After the second bag (of dog biscuits) tumbled out, I realized my mistake. She had left two kinds of treats for my dog. I was very glad that I realized my mistake in time and did not eat the dog treats!

Moral: since these biscuits look like people cookies, do not confuse these "chipped" beef jerky "cookies" for dogs with chocolate chip cookies for people!

Gourmet Dog Biscuits

"CHIPPED" BEEF JERKY DOG BISCUITS

1 ½ cups unbleached flour
1 cup whole wheat flour
¼ cup nonfat dry milk
1 egg, slightly beaten
⅓ cup vegetable oil
½ cup water
about 4 (4" x ¾") beef jerky strips dog treats - torn or crumbled into ¼ cup of ¼" pieces

1. Stir together the first three ingredients in a large bowl. Add the egg, then add the oil and water. Blend slightly.
2. Add the crumbled beef jerky to the dough.
3. Stir with a wooden spoon until well blended. Then knead the dough with your hands to create a smooth texture.
4. Roll the dough ¼ inch thick on a well-floured board. (Dust the rolling pin with flour, as necessary.) Use a 2 ½" round cookie cutter to cut out the biscuits. Place the biscuits about ½ inch apart on lightly greased cookie sheets.
5. Bake in a pre-heated 300 degree oven for about 45 minutes to one hour. The biscuits should be lightly browned on the top and bottom. Remove from oven and let cool completely.

Store in an airtight container (clearly marked "for the dog") in the refrigerator.

MAKES: ABOUT 2 DOZEN - 2" ROUND BISCUITS

While most dogs are crazy about liver, I am not that fond of it......so this is as close as I come to cooking with liver.

However, I think that this recipe will please most of the canine connoisseurs.

Gourmet Dog Biscuits

LIVER SNACKS DOG BISCUITS

1 cup raw chicken livers
1 ½ cups unbleached flour
1 ½ cups whole wheat flour
½ cup cornmeal
⅛ cup nonfat dry milk
1 egg, slightly beaten
1 cup of water

1. Boil the chicken livers in water in a small saucepan until well cooked. Remove from heat, drain the water and let the livers cool slightly. Then put the livers into a blender and puree until smooth.
2. Stir together the dry ingredients in a large bowl. Add the egg, blended liver, and water; stir until well blended. The dough should be very stiff; if not, add a little more flour. Knead the dough with your hands to thoroughly blend in the liver and create a smooth texture.
3. Roll the dough ¼ inch thick. (It helps if the "top" and "bottom" of the dough are lightly floured.) Use the cookie cutter to cut out the biscuits. Place the biscuits about ½ inch apart on lightly greased cookie sheets.
4. Bake in a pre-heated 350 degree oven for about 30 to 45 minutes. The biscuits should be lightly browned and they should not be moist inside. Turn the oven off and let the biscuits stay inside without opening the oven door for five hours, or overnight, to let them harden.

Store in an airtight container in the refrigerator.

MAKES: ABOUT 4 DOZEN - 3" x 1" BISCUITS.

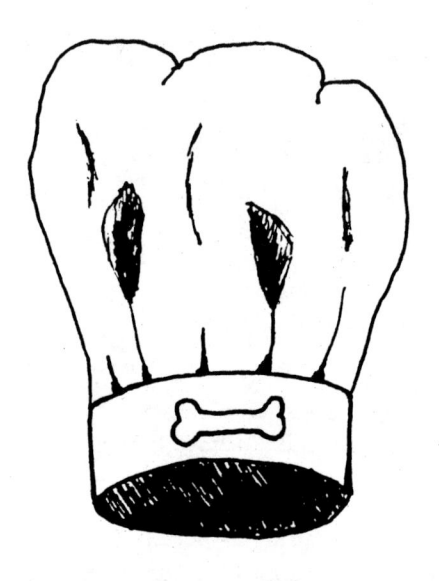

The addition of spinach adds an interesting accent to these biscuits. They look and smell so wholesome.

Gourmet Dog Biscuits

VEGETABLE-BEEF FLAVOR DOG BISCUITS

1 ½ cups unbleached flour
1 ½ cups whole wheat flour
½ cup cornmeal
⅛ cup nonfat dry milk
½ cup frozen chopped spinach, thawed (measure after excess liquid is squeezed out)
1 cup beef broth
1 egg, slightly beaten

1. Stir together the dry ingredients in a large bowl.
2. Combine the spinach and broth in a mixing bowl; then add the broth/spinach mixture and egg gradually to the flour mixture, stirring with a wooden spoon to mix well. The dough should be very stiff; if not, add a little more flour. Knead the dough with your hands to create a smooth texture.
3. Roll the dough ¼ inch thick. (It helps if the "top" and "bottom" of the dough are lightly floured.) Use the cookie cutter to cut out the biscuits. Place the biscuits about ½ inch apart on lightly greased cookie sheets.
4. Bake in a pre-heated 350 degree oven for about 45 minutes to one hour. The biscuits should be lightly browned and they should not be moist inside. Turn the oven off and let the biscuits stay inside without opening the oven door for five hours, or overnight, to let them harden.
5. Remove any excess, dried spinach from the edges of the biscuits by gently breaking off the spinach after the biscuits have cooled.

Store in an airtight container.

MAKES: ABOUT 4 DOZEN - 3" x 1" BISCUITS.

SPECIALTY FLAVORS

These biscuits are brushed with a "barbecue sauce" before baking. In addition to the flavor, the sauce adds a deep red barbecue color to the biscuits.

The sauce tends to make the biscuits a little bit sticky, so I keep them in the refrigerator.

Be sure to use a clean pastry brush to apply the "barbecue sauce."

Gourmet Dog Biscuits

BARBECUE-FLAVOR DOG BISCUITS

1 ½ cups unbleached flour
1 ½ cups whole wheat flour
½ cup cornmeal
⅛ cup nonfat dry milk
1 egg, slightly beaten
1 to 1 ¼ cups of beef broth

Sauce: *¼ cup catsup*
1 tablespoon brown sugar
one dash each: garlic powder, chili powder, paprika

1. Stir together the first four ingredients in a large bowl. Add the egg, then add the broth gradually, stirring with a wooden spoon. The dough should be very stiff; if not, add a little more flour. Knead the dough with your hands to create a smooth texture.
2. Roll the dough ¼ inch thick. (It helps if the "top" and "bottom" of the dough are lightly floured.) Use the cookie cutter to cut out the biscuits. Place the biscuits about ½ inch apart on lightly greased cookie sheets.
3. Combine the catsup, brown sugar, garlic powder, chili powder and paprika in a small bowl and mix well. Brush sauce lightly (with a clean pastry brush) on the top of the biscuits.
4. Bake in a pre-heated 350 degree oven for about 40 minutes to one hour. The biscuits should be lightly browned and they should not be moist inside. Keep an eye on them so the sauce does not burn. Turn the oven off and let the biscuits stay inside without opening the oven door for five hours, or overnight, to let them harden.

Store in an airtight container in the refrigerator.

MAKES: ABOUT 4 DOZEN - 3" x 1" BISCUITS.

Cheese is one of Baron's favorite things. Using parmesan cheese is a very easy way to add a cheesy flavor to the dog biscuits.

Gourmet Dog Biscuits

CHEESE-FLAVOR DOG BISCUITS

1 ½ cups unbleached flour
1 ½ cups whole wheat flour
½ cup cornmeal
¼ cup grated parmesan cheese (sold in a green container)
⅜ cup nonfat dry milk
1 egg, slightly beaten
1 to 1 ¼ cups of water or broth

1. Stir together the dry ingredients in a large bowl. Add the egg, then add the water or broth gradually, stirring with a wooden spoon. The dough should be very stiff; if not, add a little more flour. Knead the dough with your hands to create a smooth texture.
2. Roll the dough ¼ inch thick. (It helps if the "top" and "bottom" of the dough are lightly floured.) Use the cookie cutter to cut out the biscuits. Place the biscuits about ½ inch apart on lightly greased cookie sheets.
3. Bake in a pre-heated 350 degree oven for about 45 minutes to one hour. The biscuits should be lightly browned and they should not be moist inside. Turn the oven off and let the biscuits stay inside without opening the oven door for five hours, or overnight, to let them harden.

Store in an airtight container in the refrigerator.

MAKES: ABOUT 5 DOZEN - 3" x 1" BISCUITS.

Garlic-flavored dog biscuits are one of Baron's favorites. I haven't gotten close enough to tell whether or not they give him "garlic breath."

Be sure to use garlic powder and <u>not</u> garlic salt!

Gourmet Dog Biscuits

GARLIC DOG BISCUITS

1 ½ cups unbleached flour
1 ½ cups whole wheat flour
½ cup cornmeal
⅛ cup nonfat dry milk
⅛ to ¼ teaspoon garlic powder (not garlic salt!)
1 egg, slightly beaten
1 to 1 ¼ cups of water or broth

1. Stir together the dry ingredients in a large bowl. Add the egg, then add the water or broth gradually, stirring with a wooden spoon. The dough should be very stiff; if not, add a little more flour. Knead the dough with your hands to create a smooth texture.
2. Roll the dough ¼ inch thick. (It helps if the "top" and "bottom" of the dough are lightly floured.) Use the cookie cutter to cut out the biscuits. Place the biscuits about ½ inch apart on lightly greased cookie sheets.
3. Bake in a pre-heated 350 degree oven for about 45 minutes to one hour. The biscuits should be lightly browned and they should not be moist inside. Turn the oven off and let the biscuits stay inside without opening the oven door for five hours, or overnight, to let them harden.

Store in an airtight container.

MAKES: ABOUT 4 DOZEN - 3" x 1" BISCUITS.

These are the biscuits that Baron's "Grandma" makes for him. These dog biscuits are softer than some of the other varieties in this book.

If your dog doesn't like crunchier biscuits, this may be the recipe to try!

Note that these biscuits are baked at a slightly lower temperature than many of the other varieties.

Gourmet Dog Biscuits

"GRANDMA'S" DOG BISCUITS

½ cup unbleached flour
2 cups whole wheat flour
¼ cup nonfat dry milk
2 tablespoons brown sugar
1 egg, slightly beaten
½ cup water
½ cup vegetable oil

1. Stir together the dry ingredients in a large bowl. Add the egg, then add the water and oil. Stir with a wooden spoon until well blended. Then knead the dough with your hands to create a smooth texture. The mixture will be quite oily; if it is not stiff enough to roll out, add a little more flour.
2. Roll the dough ¼ inch thick. (It helps if the "top" and "bottom" of the dough are lightly floured.) Use the cookie cutter to cut out the biscuits. Place the biscuits about ½ inch apart on lightly greased cookie sheets.
3. Bake in a pre-heated 300 degree oven for 45 minutes to one hour. The biscuits should be golden brown and they should not be moist inside. Remove from oven and let cool completely.

Store in an airtight container in the refrigerator.

MAKES: ABOUT 4 DOZEN - 3" x 1" BISCUITS.

I worked to create a way that Baron could enjoy the flavor of pizza in his biscuits. This recipe seems to fill the bill. The spices include the key flavors of pizza. The parmesan adds the cheese flavor.

Gourmet Dog Biscuits

PIZZA-FLAVOR DOG BISCUITS

1 ½ cups unbleached flour
1 ½ cups whole wheat flour
½ cup cornmeal
¼ cup grated parmesan cheese (sold in a green container)
⅛ cup nonfat dry milk
2 teaspoons dried oregano
1 teaspoon dried basil
¼ teaspoon garlic powder (not garlic salt)
1 egg, slightly beaten
1 to 1 ¼ cups of water

1. Stir together the dry ingredients in a large bowl. Add the egg, then add the water gradually, stirring with a wooden spoon. The dough should be very stiff; if not, add a little more flour. Knead the dough with your hands to create a smooth texture.
2. Roll the dough ¼ inch thick. (It helps if the "top" and "bottom" of the dough are lightly floured.) Use the cookie cutter to cut out the biscuits. Place the biscuits about ½ inch apart on lightly greased cookie sheets.
3. Bake in a pre-heated 350 degree oven for about 45 minutes to one hour. The biscuits should be lightly browned and they should not be moist inside. Turn the oven off and let the biscuits stay inside without opening the oven door for five hours, or overnight, to let them harden.

Store in an airtight container in the refrigerator.

MAKES: ABOUT 5 DOZEN - 3" x 1" BISCUITS.

ADDITIONAL PRODUCTS

GOURMET DOG BISCUITS cookbook
A Cookbook of Tasty Treats for Your Favorite Fido

This 80-page softcover book contains 25 recipes for treats which are easy to make, inexpensive and wholesome. Flavors include garlic, apple-cinnamon, barbecue, liver, peanut butter and banana.
Price: $13.90 ($11.95 + $1.95 shipping) $15.90 outside the U.S.

HOWL-IDAY DOG BISCUITS cookbook
A Cookbook of Dog Treats for Every Season

This 104-page softcover book contains 29 tasty dog treat recipes for every season. Flavors include Yappy New Year Bone Bones™, Pumpkin Spice, "Candy Cane", Pupsicles, Beg-els™ and More!
Price: $11.90 ($9.95 + $1.95 shipping) $13.90 outside the U.S.

GOURMET CAT TREATS cookbook
A Cookbook of Tasty Treats for Your Favorite Cat

This 72-page softcover book contains 18 recipes for cat treats including catnip, cheese, chicken, fish, and liver flavors.
Price: $11.90 ($9.95 + $1.95 shipping) $13.90 outside the U.S.

DOG PARTY HANDBOOK
The Ultimate Guide for Hosting A Canine Celebration

This 28-page softcover handbook is packed with clever ideas, tasty recipes (for people and dogs) and fun games. Have a great time at your dog's party with Hot (Diggity) Dog Biscuits, Bobbing for Biscuits, "Dog Bone" Party Invitations & lots more!
Price: $9.90 ($7.95 + $1.95 shipping) $11.90 outside the U.S.

To Order: Use order form in this book, or specify book(s) ordered and send name & mailing address with a check or money order in U.S. Funds made payable to CLOUD K9 to:

CLOUD K9®
P.O. Box 190195
St. Louis, MO 63119 USA

Visit www.cloudk9.com for a wide variety of Dog Bone Cookie Cutters & Cookie Cutters in over 75 Dog Breeds!

Prices subject to change without notice.

ORDER FORM

ITEM	QUANTITY	PRICE	TOTAL
Gourmet Dog Biscuits Cookbook		$11.95 ($13.95 outside the U.S.)	
Howl-iday Dog Biscuits Cookbook		$9.95 ($11.95 outside the U.S.)	
Gourmet Cat Treats Cookbook		$9.95 ($11.95 outside the U.S.)	
Dog Party Handbook		$7.95 ($9.95 outside the U.S.)	
Shipping & Handling		$1.95 for EACH book	
		TOTAL	

Please send check or money order (in U.S. Funds) to:

Cloud K9 ®
P.O. Box 190195
St. Louis, MO 63119

Send to:

_____
Name

_____
Address

_____
City   State   ZIP CODE

(Make check payable to: Cloud K9)

NOTES

Gourmet Dog Biscuits

Index

Apple-Cinnamon, 19

Apple-Raisin, 21

Banana, 23

Banana-Peanut Butter, 51

Barbecue-Flavor, 67

Bouillon,
  substitute for broth, 9

Carob-Peanut Butter, 45

Carob Temptations, 47

Cheese-Flavor, 69

"Chipped" Beef Jerky, 59

Cookie Cutters,
  types of, 8

Dill Weed, 37

Garlic, 71

"Grandma's", 73

Herb Medley, 39

Liver Snacks, 61

"Nice" Spice, 31

Oatmeal-Cinnamon, 33

Orange, 25

Parsley, 41

Peanut Butter, 53

Peanut Butter & Jelly, 55

Pizza-Flavor, 75

Rye, 15

Tropical, 27

Vegetable-Beef Flavor, 63

Whole Wheat, 13

ABOUT THE AUTHOR

Carole Horstmeyer is a craft expert and animal lover who shares her ideas on TV and in classes. Her inspiration to create is based on her belief that crafting and cooking should be fun and easy. She resides in St. Louis.

She is also author of *Howl-iday Dog Biscuits: A Cookbook of Dog Treats for Every Season; Gourmet Cat Treats: A Cookbook of Tasty Treats for Your Favorite Cat* and *Dog Party Handbook! The Ultimate Guide for Hosting a Canine Celebration.*

Baron (Madeka's Baron Hans von Solo, CGC, CD, CDX), a long-haired German Shepherd, enjoyed his role as recipe consultant for this book.

He has earned his CD obedience title (winning Second and Third Place), and his CDX (winning Second Place).